HEWLETT-WOODMERE PUBLIC LIBRARY
HEWLETT, NEW YORK

T4-ADM-146

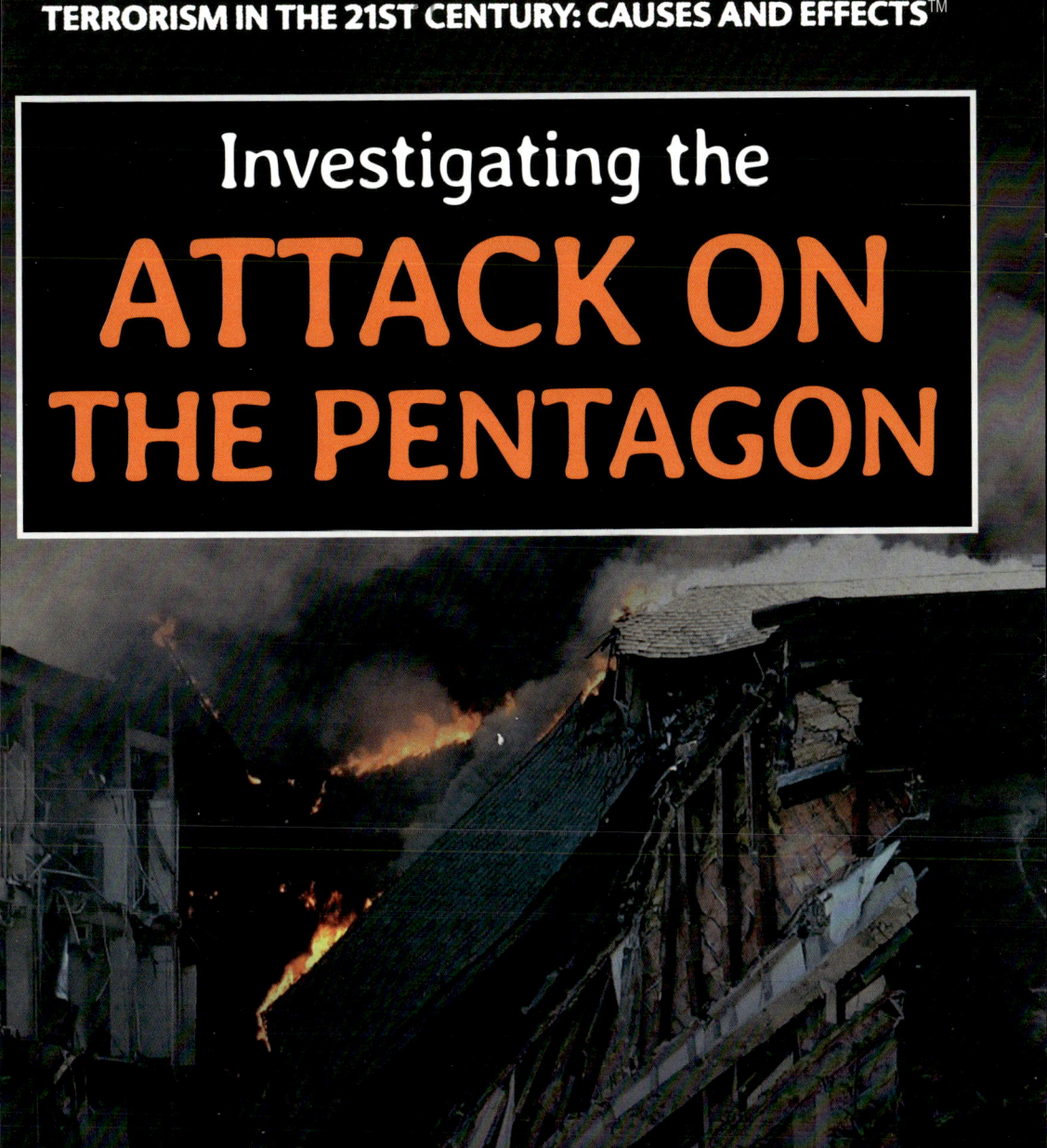

TERRORISM IN THE 21ST CENTURY: CAUSES AND EFFECTS™

Investigating the ATTACK ON THE PENTAGON

Published in 2018 by The Rosen Publishing Group, Inc.
29 East 21st Street, New York, NY 10010

Copyright © 2018 by The Rosen Publishing Group, Inc.

First Edition

All rights reserved. No part of this book may be reproduced in any form without permission in writing from the publisher, except by a reviewer.

Library of Congress Cataloging-in-Publication Data

Names: Koya, Lena, author. | Gard, Carolyn, co-author.
Title: Investigating the attack on the pentagon / Lena Koya and Carolyn Gard.
Description: New York: Rosen Publishing, 2017. | Series: Terrorism in the 21st century: causes and effects | Includes bibliographical references and index.
Identifiers: ISBN 9781508174530 (library bound)
Subjects: LCSH: September 11 Terrorist Attacks, 2001–Juvenile literature. | Pentagon (Va.)–Juvenile literature. | Terrorism–United States–Juvenile literature.
Classification: LCC HV6432.7 K69 2017 | DDC 973.931–dc23

Manufactured in the United States of America

On the cover: The Pentagon burns following the crash of Flight 77 on September 11, 2001.

3 1327 00657 6813

Contents

Introduction...4

CHAPTER ONE
The History of the Pentagon..................................6

CHAPTER TWO
Osama bin Laden and al-Qaeda............................14

CHAPTER THREE
Planning the Attack..23

CHAPTER FOUR
The Attack on the Pentagon................................30

CHAPTER FIVE
The Recovery and Investigation...........................39

CHAPTER SIX
Rebuilding..46

Timeline..53
Glossary..55
For More Information..56
For Further Reading..59
Bibliography...60
Index...62

Introduction

Located in Arlington, Virginia, just over the border with Washington, DC, the Pentagon is one of the largest office buildings in the world. The squat, five-sided building houses over twenty-five thousand employees who work for the United States Department of Defense. But these are not just any employees and the Pentagon is not just any building. The Department of Defense plays an important role in the US government and oversees all national security as well as all military branches. Some of the most important military officials in the nation work there. As such, the Pentagon is a symbol of American military might. There is no doubt that this is why it became a target for terrorists on September 11, 2001.

September 11 was a bright and sunny Tuesday morning. But, at the Pentagon that morning, many people were glued to the television screens in their offices. Two planes had just been hijacked by terrorists and flown into the World Trade Center in New York, causing great destruction and loss of life. Pentagon employees were shocked, but they never thought that they would be attacked next. Even if they were, the Pentagon was surely the safest place to be. But they were wrong.

At 9:37 a.m., American Airlines Flight 77 was flown directly into the Pentagon. The impact of the airplane caused a fireball that rose high above the building. Fire raged inside and, eventually, the top floors of the section of the Pentagon that had been hit would collapse. Many people—including top military officials and civilians—rushed from the building to escape the flames. Many did not escape the devastating attack, however, and 189 people died that day.

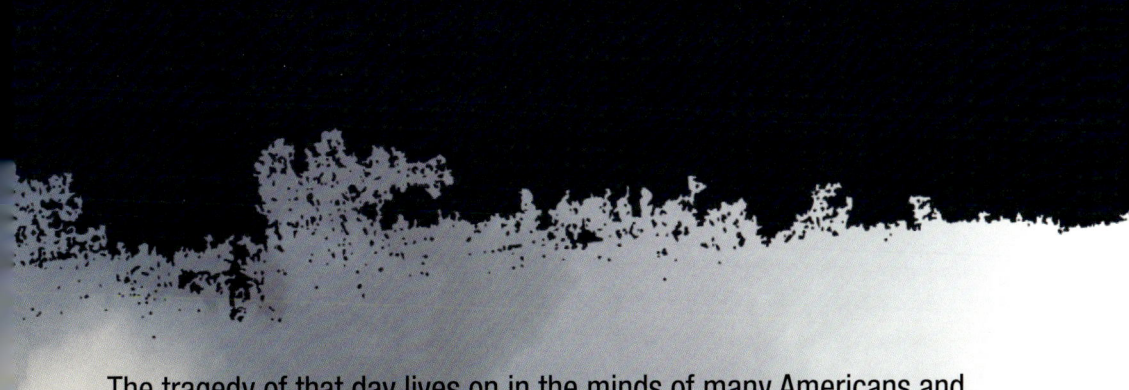

The tragedy of that day lives on in the minds of many Americans and those who were lost that day continue to be mourned. The Pentagon Memorial for victims of the September 11 attacks opened in 2008 and features a bench for each victim in the park facing the building. The project to rebuild the Pentagon, called the Phoenix Project after the mythological bird that rises from the ashes, was officially completed one year after the attack, on September 11, 2002. Indeed, while we continue to remember the tragedy of that day, we also remember the heroism of first responders and average citizens and the strength of a nation that refused to cower and, instead, perseveres.

The Pentagon, located in Arlington, Virginia, houses twenty-five thousand employees who work for the US Department of Defense.

CHAPTER ONE

The History of the Pentagon

Just prior to World War II, the United States War Department consisted of twenty-four thousand employees scattered across seventeen different buildings in Washington, DC, and Virginia. Then came the expanding conflict in Europe and the United States's expanding role in it. By 1941, the US Army alone had grown from 270,000 employees to 1.4 million employees. The department, along with other booming departments, could no longer fit into their headquarters.

The spread-out quarters also led to serious delays in both information gathering and decision making. At a time when Adolf Hitler was threatening to move into Africa, and the United States was entering a global war with devastating effects, efficiency in the military became essential.

Drafting Plans

Brigadier General Brehon Somervell, who had headed the construction division of the War Department, suggested that the country needed a single building to house the entire War Department and its staff. His idea interested both the War Department and Congress.

The Pentagon was built to house the US War Department's employees in a period of expansion at the beginning of World War II.

For several months, the War Department had been looking for a place to build temporary structures to house its growing staff. Congress had approved the funds for this move, but with the restriction that the structures be located in the District of Columbia. Such a large site didn't exist within the city limits. There was, however, a perfect site in Virginia. Arlington Farms lay across the Potomac River from Washington. The federal government already owned the land.

The tract of land has an interesting and patriotic history. In 1778, John Parke Custis, a stepson of George Washington, bought the land. Custis's granddaughter married Robert E. Lee and brought the land into the Lee

Brigadier General Brehon Somervell, who headed the construction division of the US War Department, took a lead role in building the Pentagon.

family. In 1883, the federal government bought the land from the Lee estate for $150,000.

In July of 1941, Somervell discussed his idea with Representative Clifton Woodrun of Virginia. Woodrun was a member of the House Appropriations Committee and headed the subcommittee that considered construction projects. Woodrun asked Somervell for detailed drawings. Somervell wasted no time. He immediately got engineers and architects and gave them five days to come up with plans for a building. Somervell wanted the building to be fireproof, air-conditioned, able to house forty-thousand people, no more than three stories, and have no elevators.

The drafters worked through the weekend. To make the building as efficient as possible they chose a pentagon shape. A five-sided building wasn't totally new; many of the country's early forts were pentagons. The design consisted of two rings with an inner courtyard. Connections between the rings made each wing look like a comb. The building would be 5.1 million square feet (4.7 million square meters), twice the area of the Empire State Building. The cost to build it would be $35 million.

Many people objected to the design. They argued that the building was too big for the local water and sewer facilities, it cost too much, it wasn't in Washington, the location would mar the view of the city from Arlington National Cemetery, and the building would certainly not be used after the war. These objections were overruled when President Franklin D. Roosevelt gave his approval to the project. On July 28, 1941, a little over a month after Somervell started on his design, Congress appropriated the money to build the Pentagon.

President Roosevelt signed the bill allocating the money. However, he wanted the location changed to preserve the view from the cemetery. Although the new site was only ten feet (three meters) above the level of the river and would require more construction, Somervell agreed to the change. Roosevelt also wanted the size of the building reduced by half and to have only twenty thousand employees. After the war, the building would be used to store records.

Construction

Ground was broken for the Pentagon on September 11, 1941. An old airplane hangar on the site became the headquarters for the hundreds of drafters and architects who worked on the building. Because the construction was a rush job, the designing and building work went on together. In order to keep up with the building progress the architects made new drawings every night. The machines for reproducing prints ran twenty-four hours a day. They put out twelve thousand to thirty thousand prints a week.

As the planning went on, some of the specifications changed. The building became five stories with five rings. Corridors connected the rings, and the spacing between them let natural light into the building. Many building materials were scarce because they were needed for the war effort. The designs used reinforced concrete instead of steel for the walls. This saved thirty-eight thousand tons of steel—enough steel to build a battleship. The materials for the concrete came from the Potomac River itself. Barges brought the sand and gravel from the river to the building site. There they were fed into trucks and mixed on the way to the construction site. The use of ramps instead of elevators saved more steel. The only substitution that proved to be unwise was the use of asbestos in ducts to save steel. Years later the disease-causing asbestos had to be removed.

The five-sided ring design fit the criteria of efficiency. The farthest a person might have to walk from one part of the building to another is

FACTS AND FIGURES ABOUT THE PENTAGON

The Pentagon is one of the world's largest office buildings. Here are some facts to illustrate just how large the Pentagon is:

Total land area	583 acres (236 hectares)
Building area	34 acres (14 ha)
Area of center courtyard	5 acres (2 ha)
Floor area	6,500,000 square feet (600,000 sq. m)
Stairways	131
Escalators	19
Elevators	13
Restrooms	284
Windows	7,748
Employees (2014)	23,000

1,800 feet (5,486 meters), about a third of a mile. Even walking slowly, a person could do this in less than ten minutes.

At the time the Pentagon was built, segregation of blacks and whites was common, especially in the South. Although separate restrooms and lunchrooms were built for blacks and whites in the Pentagon, the "Whites" and "Coloreds" signs were never put up.

Initial construction on the Pentagon lasted from 1941 until 1943.

When the Japanese attacked Pearl Harbor in December of 1941, the pace of construction at the Pentagon increased. In April 1942, less than eight months after the ground breaking, three hundred employees moved into the first completed section. The Pentagon was officially completed on January 15, 1943. About thirty-three thousand people worked in the building.

The Pentagon's Continued Importance

After World War II, the United States still needed a large military presence to deal with the unstable world during the Cold War years (1946–1991). Any thoughts that the Pentagon would no longer be needed were quickly forgotten. As the needs of the military grew, changes were made to the Pentagon. Open spaces were closed off to make offices. Because of security reasons and because noxious fumes seeped into the building, the bus and taxi tunnels in the building were made into offices. The corridors, which were bare at the beginning, were decorated with state flags, US flags, presidential photos, and Medal of Honor heroes. Two dozen special halls were dedicated to individuals who served their country.

In light of the September 11 attacks, two historical comments about the Pentagon proved to be prophetic. In 1941 Gilmore Clarke, the head of the Washington, DC, Commission on Fine Arts said that, "The Pentagon presented the largest target in the world for enemy bombs." In 1968, Ada Louise Huxtable, the architecture critic of the *New York Times*, wrote, "The best thing about the building ... is that it is horizontal, not vertical: City planners, corporate clients, and architects still might ponder the usefulness of that lesson."

CHAPTER TWO

Osama bin Laden and al-Qaeda

In the Middle East, a terrorist organization under the leadership of a wealthy Saudi named Osama bin Laden was rapidly gaining members. Bin Laden inherited a large fortune from his father when he died and moved from Saudi Arabia to Pakistan. While there, he supported Muslims who fought against Soviets in neighboring Afghanistan. Then, in the late 1980s, bin Laden founded al-Qaeda, which means "the base" in Arabic. Bin Laden wanted al-Qaeda to fight against Western targets (whether governments or civilians) who, according to him, oppressed Muslims and lived sinful lives. Al-Qaeda would quickly become one of the largest terrorist organizations in the world.

After the war in Afghanistan, bin Laden returned to Saudi Arabia. He hated the United States because he believed that it stood for moral depravity and anti-Muslim ideas. He argued that the United States was not governed in a way that fit his extremist Islamic views.

Another problem bin Laden had with the United States was that he believed it supported infidel (rejecting his religious faith) countries and organizations. These included Saudi Arabia, Egypt, Israel, and the United Nations. Finally, bin Laden resented the involvement of the United States in the 1990 Gulf War and in Operation Restore Hope in Somalia in 1992 and 1993. Bin Laden felt snubbed when the Saudi Arabian government turned

Osama bin Laden founded the terrorist organization al-Qaeda in the late 1980s.

down his proposal to remove American forces from the Arabian Peninsula and let bin Laden and his army protect the country.

The Evolution of al-Qaeda

Osama bin Laden decided to use terrorism to make the Middle East a Muslim stronghold. He used al-Qaeda to spread terrorism around the world. The headquarters of al-Qaeda remained in Afghanistan and Pakistan until 1991, when bin Laden was expelled from Saudi Arabia and moved to Sudan.

Meanwhile, Pakistani officials were upset with bin Laden's followers, who were living in tents on the Pakistan-Afghanistan border. Their militant views caused trouble. Bin Laden flew about five hundred of these veterans of the Afghan war to the Sudan.

Many of these al-Qaeda members weren't happy. There was no jihad (religious crusade) to fight in Sudan. According to Simon Reeve's book on terrorism, *The New Jackals*, Mamdouh Mahmud Salim was an associate of bin Laden and was arrested by the German police in September of 1998. Salim told his interrogators that there were three types of men in al-Qaeda: "People who had no success in life, had nothing in their heads, and wanted to join just to keep from falling on their noses … people who loved their religion but had no idea what their religion meant," and people with "nothing in their heads but to fight and solve all the problems of the world with battles."

Bin Laden set up businesses in Sudan through which al-Qaeda's work could be done without attracting attention. These businesses were involved in investments, agriculture, construction, and transportation. The companies earned money for the group. They also provided a cover for the purchase and transfer of explosives, weapons, and chemicals. By pretending they were on company business, al-Qaeda officials could travel outside Sudan to plan terrorist attacks.

Osama bin Laden and al-Qaeda sponsored training camps for terrorists. Bin Laden's wealth purchased arms for these trainees. One shipment of firearms is supposed to have cost $15 million. In the camps the fighters learned to use firearms, explosives, chemical weapons, and other weapons of mass destruction. The camps also planned attacks against US targets. They conducted experiments in the use of chemical and biological weapons.

Next, bin Laden turned his attention to the development of the international aspect of al-Qaeda. He opened an office of the Advice and Reformation Committee in London. The committee worked to make Saudi Arabia conform to strict Islamic law. Bin Laden established ties with Yemen and Albania. Both of these countries had militant and oppressed Muslims. Bin Laden bought businesses in both countries and encouraged militancy among the Muslims.

After the February 1993 bombing of the World Trade Center, Federal Bureau of Investigation (FBI) agents found connections between the bombers and Osama bin Laden. From then on the Central Intelligence Agency (CIA) kept close track of his activities. In January of 1996, the CIA set up a special bin Laden task force. More than eleven agencies tracked his movements. This became the most expensive investigation into a single terrorist ever. In 1996, pressure from the United States, Egypt, and Saudi Arabia forced Sudan to expel bin Laden. He went to Afghanistan, where he got support from Pakistan and from Mullah Mohamed Omar, the leader of the Taliban.

The Taliban, the ruling group in Afghanistan on September 11, 2001, is a group of extremist, fundamentalist Muslims who took control of the

Investigating the ATTACK ON THE PENTAGON

country in 1996 and set up a government with harsh laws. Many of these laws put strict restrictions on women by making them cover their faces when they went out and preventing them from getting an education or working.

Structure and Previous Activity

Al-Qaeda is an umbrella organization that connects several terrorist organizations operating in many countries. These include the Egyptian Islamic Jihad, the Islamic Group, and jihad groups in several other

The 1993 World Trade Center bombing brought al-Qaeda to the attention of the FBI and other US intelligence agencies.

countries. The groundwork is done through "cells." Each cell is a group of about ten to twelve men. Cells operate in at least sixty countries. By the early 2000s, the FBI gathered evidence of four or five al-Qaeda cells in the United States. All the group members entered the United States legally.

The cells are financed by the drug trade, by taking money from individual donors and Islamic charities (either legitimate ones or ones set up to funnel money to al-Qaeda), and through criminal activities. Although most of bin Laden's fortune was gone by the time of the attacks, the cells he set up became self-sufficient. The members work for a reward from their god, Allah, not for financial gain. A secret society like al-Qaeda depends on trust. The nineteen hijackers of the four airplanes used in the September 11 attacks completed terrorist training in Afghanistan. Many were school friends, some had lived together for years, and others were related by family ties. These ties, which outsiders could not see, kept the terrorist network together.

Cell members are highly disciplined and patient. After September 11, neighbors of some of the hijackers remembered that the men kept to themselves and always traveled together. When authorities retraced the steps of the hijackers they found that some of them had waited five years for their deadly missions. Estimates of the number of al-Qaeda members worldwide range from approximately twenty-five thousand to forty thousand as of 2014.

Al-Qaeda has two levels of government. One level encourages militants to attack secular, or nonreligious, governments. These cells are given money by al-Qaeda. The details of these attacks are left up to the individual cells.

The other level of al-Qaeda is run by a *majilis al shura*, a council that approves major projects. Both bin Laden and his assistant, Muhammad

Osama bin Laden (*second from left*) is pictured with other members of al-Qaeda following the September 11 attacks.

Atef, served on the majilis al shura. Because of their level of oversight over the organization, the council forms part of al-Qaeda's central command, which has continued even following the death of bin Laden. Evidence collected by intelligence agencies suggests that this higher level of command carried out the attacks against the United States embassies in Africa, the attack on the USS *Cole*, and the September 11 attacks on the World Trade Center and Pentagon.

Al-Qaeda has not always been successful. Authorities have stopped

A NEW BREED OF TERRORISTS

At the time of the terrorist attacks in 2001, al-Qaeda represented a new breed of terrorists who remained loyal to a religious ideal rather than to a state. However, in the years since the September 11 attacks, new forms of terrorism have developed and, unfortunately, have become more commonplace. Developing from an al-Qaeda group following the 2003 war in Iraq, the Islamic State (IS) is a new breed of terrorist group that has built upon and, indeed, surpassed al-Qaeda's goals. These terrorists harbor a deep hatred for Americans and justify the killing of civilians for their religious and political goals. Just as frightening is the fact that IS has not only successfully carried out suicide attacks against civilians around the world, but they have also successfully gained large amounts of territory in Syria and Iraq, something al-Qaeda never did. As of the time of this writing, IS has lost large amounts of territory in the Middle East but continues its fight.

attempts by al-Qaeda members to assassinate Pope John Paul II in Manila, Philippines, in 1994; to bomb the capitals of the United States, Israel, and several Asian countries in 1994; to destroy several transpacific flights in 1995; and to kill President Clinton during a visit to the Philippines in 1995.

In 1998, the United States launched Tomahawk cruise missiles against bin Laden's Afghan headquarters. The attack did not result in the capture of bin Laden and may have brought more militants into al-Qaeda's fold. By late 1998, over twenty militant groups were part of al-Qaeda.

Before September 11, the United States had gained some information about al-Qaeda. A former member of the network revealed that al-Qaeda was trying to get nuclear and chemical weapons. Witnesses in other terrorism-related trials said that bin Laden had declared a fatwa, or decree, against the United States. The fatwa said that it was the duty of all Muslims to kill Americans, both military and civilian, wherever they might be found.

Around 1996, several men of Middle Eastern descent entered the United States. They lived quietly in suburbs, keeping to themselves but not arousing the suspicions of their neighbors. All too soon they would become known to every American.

CHAPTER THREE

Planning the Attack

For five years before the attack, al-Qaeda operatives carried out the earliest steps in their extensive plan. Beginning in 1996, five men who were linked to al-Qaeda received visas and moved to the United States. During this time, they lived quietly in modest apartments while seeking out flying lessons.

A reporter analyzes the visa application of September 11 terrorist Hani Hanjour.

In the spring of 1996, Hani Hanjour, a twenty-five-year-old Saudi, arrived in Hollywood, Florida. He lived with a couple who were friends of his brother. He told them he wanted to get into a flight school, but he wasn't accepted to any. In May he moved to Oakland, California.

In September of 1996, Hanjour went to Scottsdale, Arizona, a suburb of Phoenix. He took flight lessons at the CRM Flight School. The lessons cost $4,749. He took lessons for three months. In December of 1997, he went back for more lessons. Hanjour wanted a private pilot's license. His flight instructor said he was a poor pilot who didn't do his homework and missed lessons. He may have gotten a commercial pilot's license for single engine planes in Saudi Arabia in 1999.

In 1999, Hanjour moved to the United Arab Emirates. He soon returned to the United States and lived in an apartment in San Diego.

Terrorist Connections

Meanwhile, in January of 2000, another Saudi, Nawaf Alhazmi, twenty-four, and a Yemenite, Khalid Almihdhar, twenty-five, went to Malaysia. Secret police in Kuala Lumpur filmed Alhazmi and Almihdhar while the two men talked with a senior aide to Osama bin Laden. This aide was a suspect in the bombing of the USS *Cole*. The men met with other al-Qaeda members in a condominium at a resort. Alhazmi and Almihdhar told the others that they were to "kill Americans and destroy American interests and those who support America."

In the middle of January, Alhazmi and Almihdhar flew from Bangkok, Thailand, to Los Angeles. They stayed with Hanjour in San Diego. Mohamed Atta, the pilot of the plane that would crash into the north tower of the World Trade Center, often visited them.

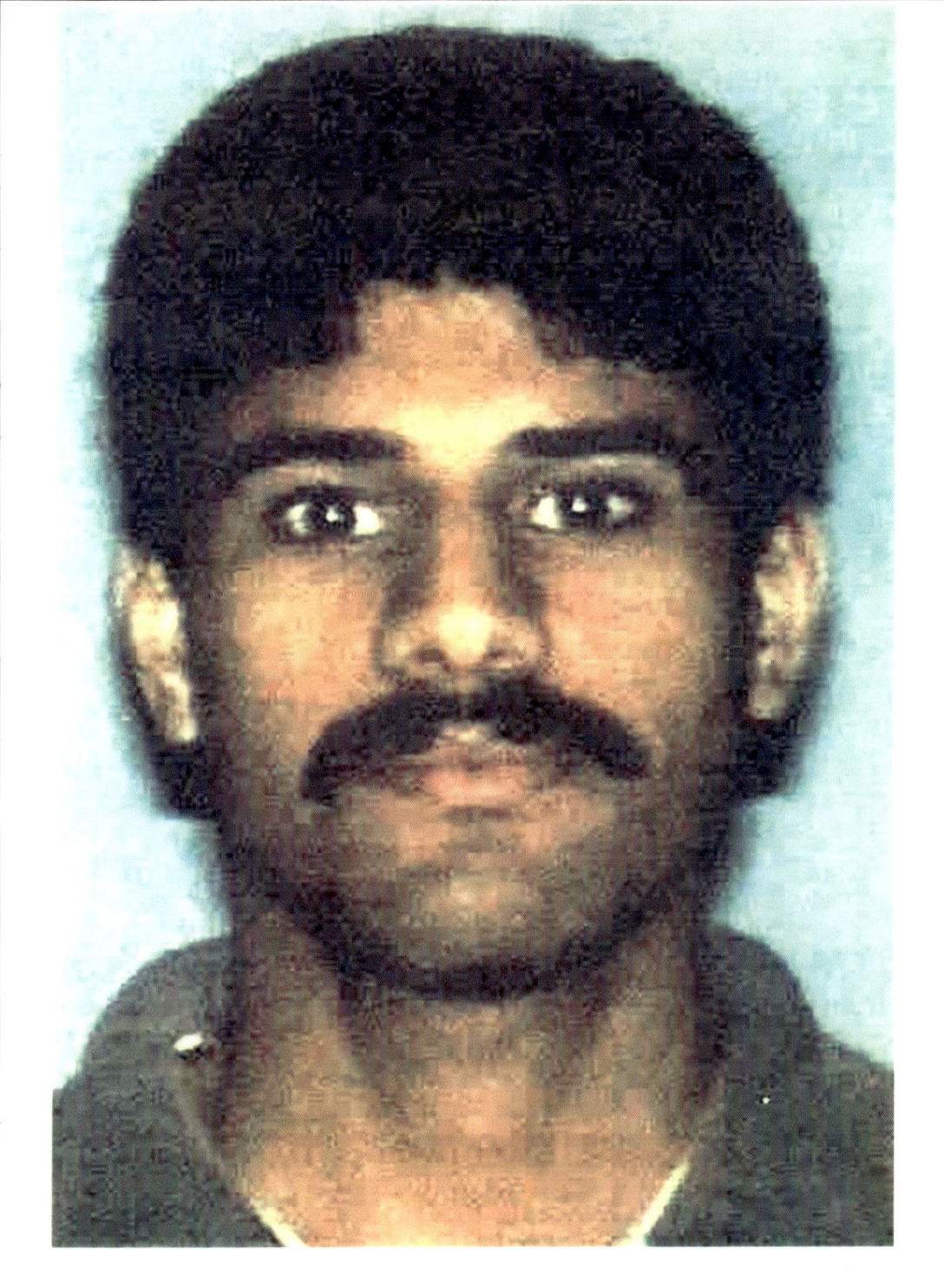

Nawaf Alhazmi

Twenty-four-year-old Nawaf Alhazmi was one of five hijackers aboard Flight 77, which crashed into the Pentagon on September 11, 2001.

In May of 2001, Alhazmi and Almihdhar took three weeks of flight training lessons at Sorbi's Flying Club in San Diego. They told the instructor that they wanted to fly Boeings, but they were restricted to a twin-engine Cessna. The men were not quick studies.

Alhazmi and Almihdhar entered the United States again on business visas in July of 2001. They gave a Marriott hotel in New York City as their address. In August the FBI put the two men on a watch list.

Final Preparations

Nawaf Alhazmi and Khalid Almihdhar went to Las Vegas in August of 2001, where they met with the four pilots who would fly the hijacked planes on September 11. The six men stayed in cheap hotels. They probably worked

THE HIJACKERS

In total, nineteen hijackers took over four planes on September 11, 2001: American Airlines Flight 77, which flew into the Pentagon; United Airlines Flights 175 and 11, which were flown into the World Trade Center; and United Airlines Flight 93, which crashed into a field in Shanksville, Pennsylvania. All the hijackers were men in their twenties and early thirties; the oldest was Mohamed Atta at age thirty-three, and the youngest Ahmed al-Haznawi and Hamza al-Ghamdi, who were both twenty. Fifteen of the nineteen hijackers were Saudi Arabian.

on details of the planned attacks. This followed the al-Qaeda pattern of keeping cells separate. The cell members only come together shortly before an attack. Ordinarily, cell members have face-to-face meetings in secure rooms, and instructions are often given in a coded language.

Hanjour kept trying to improve his piloting skills. In June of 2001, al-Qaeda sent an Algerian pilot, Lofti Raissi, to the United States to help Hanjour train on a jet simulator. The practice may not have been a lot of help. In August 2001, Hanjour flew three times with instructors at a flight school in Bowie, Maryland, outside of Washington, DC. Once again, his instructors weren't impressed with his ability. They refused to let him rent a plane.

By September 2001, Hanjour, Nawaf Alhazmi, Almihdhar, thirty-year-old Salem Alhazmi, and another Saudi, twenty-four-year-old Majed Moqed, were sharing a $280-a-week room at the Valencia Motel in Laurel, Maryland, a suburb of Washington, DC. According to neighbors, the men drove a blue Toyota and always went out together. They paid regular visits to Gold's Gym in Greenbelt, Maryland.

"The Last Night"

A document found in Nawaf Alhazmi's car titled "The Last Night" gives a glimpse of what went through the minds of the five men on September 10. The document instructs them to take a "pledge of allegiance for death and renewal of intent." They are to read and understand certain chapters in the Koran. Many times they are urged to pray to Allah and to cleanse their hearts. There is advice on how to fight and the instruction to take a shower. One of the passages that must have inspired them reads, "Smile in the face of death, oh young man! For you are on your way to the everlasting paradise!"

Al-Qaeda terrorists Mohamed Atta (*right*) and Abdulaziz al-Omari pass through security before boarding on September 11, 2001.

Boarding Flight 77

On the morning of September 11, 2001, the five men arrived at Dulles Airport in Virginia, where they boarded American Airlines Flight 77 bound for Los Angeles. In their car they left a cashier's check made out to a flight school in Phoenix, a box cutter, drawings of the cockpit of a Boeing 757, and a map of Washington, DC. Fifty-three other passengers boarded Flight 77. Among them were two staff members of the National Geographic Society, three teachers, and three students. The eight were headed to California. The three students, eleven-year-old sixth graders, had been selected to be part of a program at the Channel Islands National Marine Sanctuary near Santa Barbara, California. The program, a Sustainable Seas Expedition, let the students work with biologists to monitor ocean life and activity. The kids had also planned to kayak and hike to various study areas. The students were from middle schools in Washington, DC, and were excited to be going on this adventure. An adult who went to the airport with them said that the kids wore their National Geographic caps and marched past the check-in counter as if to say, "We're on official business."

The pilot, Charles Burlingame, who had landed wounded F-4 Phantoms on the deck of an aircraft carrier in high seas, sat at the controls. About 8:00 a.m. Eastern Standard Time, Flight 77 taxied out to the runway. It was a beautiful late summer day in Washington.

CHAPTER FOUR

The Attack on the Pentagon

At 8:19 a.m. on September 11, 2001, Flight 77 was cleared for takeoff. Air traffic control instructed the pilot to taxi his plane to runway three zero at Dulles Airport. He replied: "One two five oh

The Pentagon burns immediately following the crash of American Airlines Flight 77.

five. Runway three zero cleared for takeoff, American 77." Within one minute, Flight 77 had lifted off and began heading west across northern Virginia and West Virginia.

The tower instructed the pilot to climb to 11,000 feet (3,353 m). For the next few minutes the pilot and tower stayed in contact as Flight 77 avoided other incoming and outgoing planes. The plane climbed to 33,000 feet (10,058 m) and continued west. About twenty minutes into the flight, the control tower in Indianapolis took over from the Washington air route traffic control.

Growing Concerns

At 8:56 a.m. Flight 77 neared the Ohio-Kentucky border. The Indianapolis control tower tried to contact the pilot. After two minutes with no response, the controller called the American Airlines dispatcher. The dispatcher tried unsuccessfully to contact the plane.

The control tower had not only lost radio contact, the plane had disappeared from the radar screens. The tower alerted other control sectors to watch for the plane. At 9:09 a.m., word came that United Airlines Flight 175 had hit the World Trade Center. Suspicion must have started growing. Like Flight 77, that plane had been headed for Los Angeles.

Aboard Flight 77, the terror had started. Passengers making frantic calls to loved ones from their cell phones reported that several men with knives and box cutters had overpowered the crew and taken over the cockpit. The hijackers pushed the passengers and crew to the back of the plane. Then they turned off the transponder, the device that sends information to the control tower's radar screens. Investigators later said that action proved the hijackers had knowledge of flying a plane. The hijacker pilot, probably

Investigating the ATTACK ON THE PENTAGON

Hani Hanjour, turned the plane east, back toward Washington. As the plane neared the city it flew low over the Columbia Pike, one of the main roads that leads to the Pentagon.

The Impact

Shortly after 9:30 a.m. controllers at Dulles Airport saw an unidentified aircraft headed at high speed toward the restricted airspace around the White House. Controllers hurriedly called Reagan National Airport in Washington and the White House to warn them of the possible attack.

Secretary of Defense Donald Rumsfeld was attending a meeting on missile defense in the Pentagon. When he heard of the attacks on the World Trade Center he predicted that the United States would face another terrorist incident. He then hurried back to his office. As Rumsfeld spoke these words, Flight 77 neared the Pentagon. It was too high and going too fast. The hijacker-pilot made a difficult high-speed turn as he descended. The plane dropped 7,000 feet (2,134 m) in two minutes. At 9:38 a.m. the pilot of Flight 77 throttled up the engines. The plane carrying sixty-four passengers slammed into the Pentagon at 530 mph (853 kmh). The impact took a thirty yard by ten yard (27 m by 9 m) slice out of the building and sent a fireball sixty feet (18 m) into the air. The massive building shook.

A Vietnam veteran, who was part of a construction team working at the Pentagon was walking along the sidewalk as the aircraft approached. He heard a terrible noise. As he looked around, he saw the plane clip a couple of light poles on the way in. He fell flat, convinced that if he hadn't the plane would have hit him.

THE DAMAGE DONE

When Flight 77 crashed into the Pentagon, it was traveling 530 miles per hour (853 km/h). Because this large and powerful commercial airliner was traveling so fast at the moment of impact, it:
- Penetrated 24-inch (61-centimeter)-thick walls—6 inches (15 cm) of limestone, 8 inches (20 cm) of brick, 10 inches (25 cm) of concrete
- Went through 5-inch (13-cm) concrete floors
- Made a hole 100 feet (30 m) wide
- Damaged three of the five rings and killed 189 people

Immediate Reactions

Secretary Rumsfeld ran from his office on the opposite side of the building to the attack site. He helped put some of the injured onto stretchers. Then he went to the National Military Command Center (NMCC), located in the lower floors of the Pentagon.

From the NMCC the leaders in the Pentagon can observe and control actions by the Department of Defense anywhere in the world. The NMCC staff of about three hundred constantly monitors conditions worldwide, particularly concerning nuclear command and control and missile warning systems. Despite the smoke that seeped into the room, the staff remained in the center. The Pentagon placed the military on Threatcom Delta—the highest alert status short of war.

Donald Rumsfeld (*left*) and President George W. Bush survey the damage at the Pentagon.

Upstairs, Pentagon workers helped each other out of their offices and the building. Defense Protective Service officers directed the evacuation. Some people had to run across the burning airplane to get out. Rescue workers and employees fought their way through black smoke and heat. Throughout the Pentagon voices could be heard calling out to anyone who might still be inside. Those in the undamaged parts of the building took the time to secure classified items before leaving.

The Attack on the Pentagon

The Arlington County police and fire departments arrived and pumped water on the fire. Medical professionals driving by set up triage areas in the parking lot. Many passersby transported the injured to hospitals in their private vehicles. Helicopters flew the most seriously wounded to area hospitals. The official forces were bolstered by Fort Belvoir engineers experienced in search and rescue, FBI agents, and Federal Emergency Management Agency (FEMA) teams.

At 10:10 a.m. the part of the Pentagon next to the impact area collapsed. That half hour had given many workers a chance to escape. After the collapse firefighters and rescue workers had to wait to go back in until the portion could be stabilized.

Firefighters pour water on the impact site following the crash of Flight 77.

Investigating the ATTACK ON THE PENTAGON

By this time, much of Washington had been evacuated. This included the White House, the Capitol, all federal office buildings, the Supreme Court, and all the museums and monuments. Foreign embassies shut down, as well as international financial organizations. The exodus led to massive gridlock on the roads.

The Federal Aviation Administration (FAA) ordered all commercial and private aircraft flying in the United States to land at the nearest airport. By 10:30 a.m., F-16 and F-15 fighter planes patrolled the skies over Washington in response to reports that more hijacked planes were on the way. Two tankers were also in the area so the fighters could be refueled without landing. By the end of the day, some of the fighters had been in the air for over eight hours. Early in the afternoon five warships and two aircraft carriers left the US Naval Station in Norfolk, Virginia. Their mission was to protect the East Coast and to reduce the number of ships in the port, perhaps to avoid another Pearl Harbor.

A small crisis occurred when the cell phone network around the Pentagon overloaded. Those who could get through passed along phone numbers and messages. The fire at the building proved to be a tough problem. Materials in the roof burned and were almost impossible to get at. Pools of jet fuel ignited. At 9:30 p.m. the fire was still not under control.

A Shred of Good News

One small piece of good news was that the area of the Pentagon that Flight 77 struck had been undergoing remodeling and was not yet fully occupied. In addition, some of the renovations may have allowed more people to escape. Vertical steel beams had been placed on either side of every window, and a strong mesh material, similar to the Kevlar used in bulletproof vests, had been stretched between the steel beams to catch

Rescue workers search in the Pentagon on September 13, 2001.

debris in the event of an explosion. The windows themselves had been replaced with 1.5-inch (3.8 cm) thick panes of blast-resistant glass.

Two employees of the contractor for the renovation had been on the fifth floor of the outermost ring, about 75 feet (23 m) from the point of impact. The area immediately filled with black smoke. The two crawled

37

Investigating the ATTACK ON THE PENTAGON

on their hands and knees checking every office on the fifth floor to make sure that everyone got out. They then went down to the fourth, third, and second floors, where they again checked the offices. The contractor believed that renovations kept the structure from collapsing for a half hour. They also slowed the plane as it entered the building.

On the evening of September 11, Secretary Rumsfeld held a press conference in the Pentagon as the fire continued to burn. He said, "The Pentagon is functioning. It will be in business tomorrow."

CHAPTER FIVE

The Recovery and Investigation

Rescue workers and medical personnel worked around the clock to find and stabilize survivors and remove bodies. Rescue workers would often be forced to stop their search in order to conduct brief checks to make sure the building around them was not in immediate danger of collapsing. The final death total was a sobering 189: 64 passengers on the airplane and 125 people in the Pentagon.

Emergency workers aid the wounded immediately following the attack on the Pentagon.

Most of the fuselage of the plane stayed intact after the impact. Searchers hunting through the rubble heard signals from the plane's black box. They found the box on the Friday after the attack. Both the recorders inside had been damaged. The recorders were sent to a laboratory at the National Transportation Safety Board in Washington. Unfortunately, the technicians were not able to get any useful information from them.

Search and Rescue

The Federal Emergency Management Agency (FEMA) flew in several urban search and rescue (US&R) teams to help with the recovery. These teams coordinate the local emergency personnel into a unified force. They brief local officials on public assistance and make plans for removing the debris. To be certified by FEMA, US&R teams must meet several criteria.

AN AIRPLANE'S BLACK BOX

The black box (which is actually orange to aid the searchers) is mounted in the tail of the plane. It is made of insulated titanium to protect it from fire, impact, and water pressure. Two recorders inside the box collect over three hundred pieces of information. The cockpit data recorder registers flight crew conversations, cockpit sounds, and engine noises, while the flight data recorder registers data such as airspeed, altitude, heading, time, and latitude and longitude of the flight.

The Recovery and Investigation

The members are all certified emergency medical technicians. They can be deployed in six hours. They can sustain themselves (provide food, shelter, etc.) for seventy-two hours. Each group has sixty-two members who can fill thirty-one positions, including engineers, search specialists with trained dogs, physicians, nurses, hazard materials specialists, and communications personnel.

Once the teams got to the Pentagon they set up a base of operations. The search specialists checked blueprints and then went into the damaged area. As they went they braced areas that were in danger of collapsing. The rescuers worked on the building from the front and from

Flight 77's black box (which is actually a bright orange) was too damaged to provide useful information for investigators.

Investigating the ATTACK ON THE PENTAGON

the outside to minimize the danger of more collapsing. Then searchers with dogs went inside.

US&R teams stay at a site until it is determined that no more victims will be found alive. The last team left the Pentagon on September 22, 2001.

The Investigation

Two weeks after the attack, the FBI took control of the Pentagon site. That turned the investigation into a criminal one. As the crews went into the wreckage they examined the rubble. The loads of debris were taken to a parking lot. Crime scene technicians cataloged potential evidence. In the first two weeks workers removed over ten thousand tons of debris. Fifteen hundred people worked on the cleanup and investigation. The FBI estimated that they would be at the scene for a month going through the debris.

Three months after the attack the US Army had a more delicate task to perform. Thousands of people had left mementos on a hill overlooking the Pentagon. Wreaths, flowers, photographs, notes, teddy bears, and flags covered the ground. To protect the offerings from the weather the Army decided to store them for safekeeping and later display some in a permanent memorial. The movers took their time packing the mementos that expressed the condolences of strangers and the unity that Americans showed after the attacks.

One rumor that circulated after the attack on the Pentagon was that Flight 77 had actually been headed for the White House. Top administration officials, including Vice President Dick Cheney, thought that the White House was the primary target. They argued that the hijackers changed their minds because of the difficulty of spotting the White House since taller buildings surround it. However, the recorded flight path shows that the plane was south of the restricted air space around the White House. The Pentagon, the center of the US military, would have been just as symbolic a structure to hit as the White House.

As the cleanup efforts continued, the FBI quickly identified the hijackers. Sixteen of the nineteen men on all four planes had definite ties to Osama bin Laden. All of the pilots had been trained in the United States. More than seven thousand federal investigators worked on the investigation. They put data including phone bills, ATM receipts, fake IDs, and Islamic verse into computer databases. They hoped to find patterns that connected the hijackers with others who might have been involved in the attacks.

Additional Suspects

Several men with suspected ties to the hijackers were questioned and detained. Osama Awadallah was arrested in San Diego after FBI agents found his name and phone number in Nawaf Alhazmi's car. Lofti Raissi, the man who had supposedly given jet simulator lessons to Hanjour, was arrested in London. A third man, Faisal Michael Al Salmi, was accused of lying to the FBI about his ties to Hanjour. He was transported from Arizona to New York for questioning.

The three men pleaded innocent to any terrorist activities. Their lawyers argued that any evidence was simply coincidence. Spokespeople for various human-rights organizations worried that innocent people were being held without bail because they had the wrong last name.

On December 11, 2001, the Department of Justice brought the first indictment against a terrorist involved in the September 11 attacks. A grand jury in Virginia charged Zacarias Moussaoui, a French-born Moroccan, with conspiring with al-Qaeda and Osama bin Laden to kill thousands of innocent people on September 11. The indictment against

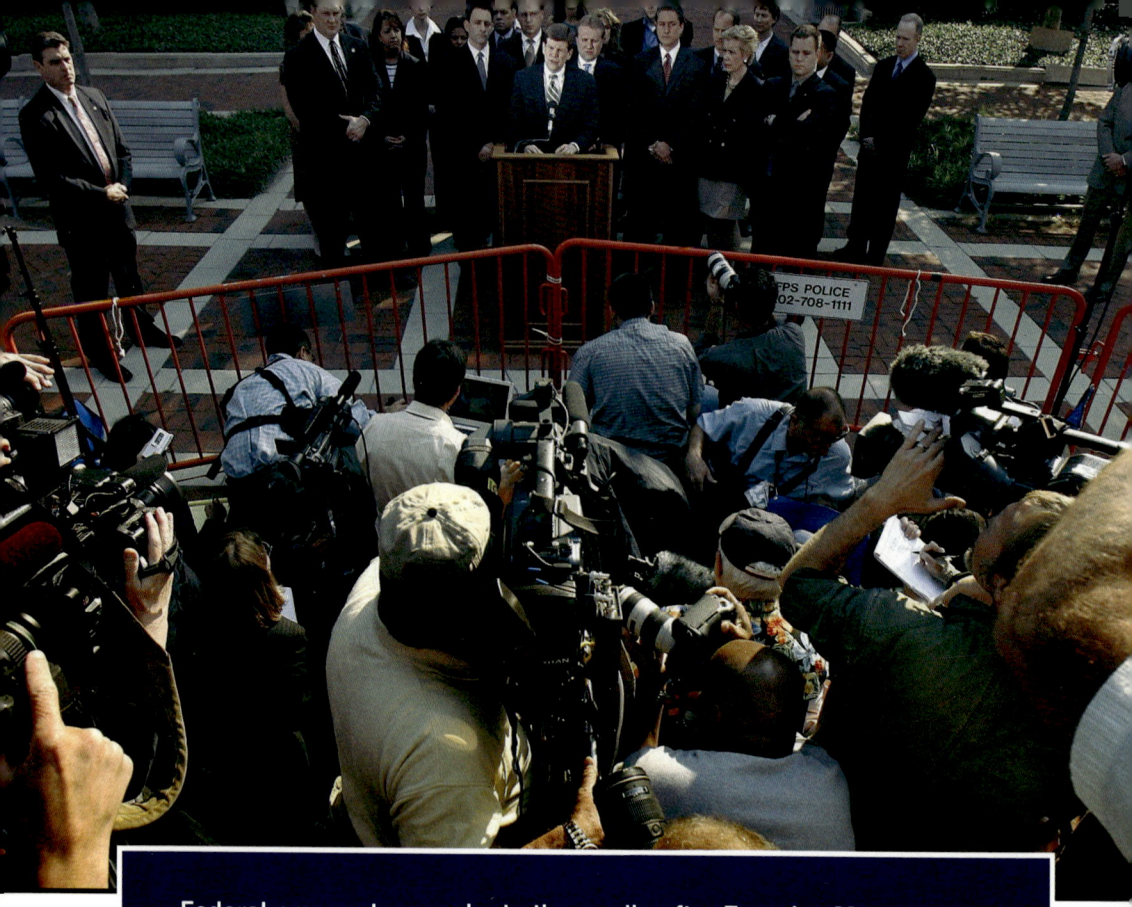

Federal prosecutors spoke to the media after Zacarias Moussaoui was sentenced to life in prison for his role in the September 11 attacks.

him places him at a terrorist camp in Afghanistan in 1998. Officials believe that Moussaoui was supposed to be the twentieth hijacker.

Moussaoui came to the United States in February of 2001 wanting to learn to fly. After he failed out of a flight school in Oklahoma he went to a flight school in Minnesota, where he paid $6,300 in cash to use flight simulators. The instructors became suspicious of the cash payments and contacted the FBI. Moussaoui was detained on August 17 for immigration violations. He has been in a jail ever since.

Some of the evidence the FBI found in Moussaoui's possession were flight manuals for the Boeing 747, a flight-simulator computer program, two knives, fighting shields, and a laptop computer. Moussaoui also had the phone number of Ramzi bin al-Shibh, a member of the Hamburg, Germany, al-Qaeda cell, who had sent money to Moussaoui. Al-Shibh had twice been denied a visa to travel to the United States.

The charges against Moussaoui ran to thirty pages, much of it showing how his actions paralleled those of the hijackers. The indictment listed six counts of conspiracy against Moussaoui: conspiracies to commit terrorism, to commit aircraft piracy, to destroy aircraft, to use weapons of mass destruction, to murder United States employees, and to destroy property. Moussaoui was eligible for the death penalty for the first four sentences.

On May 3, 2006, the jury on Moussaoui's trial reached a verdict. They found him guilty on all counts and he was subsequently sentenced to six consecutive life sentences without the possibility of parole. Moussaoui was saved from execution by only one jury member as the final jury voted him guilty of terrorism by eleven to one. The death penalty requires unanimous agreement. Since his conviction, Moussaoui has been held in a maximum security prison in Colorado.

CHAPTER SIX

Rebuilding

When Flight 77 crashed into Wedge 1 of the Pentagon, it destroyed a section of the building that had already been under renovation for four years. In fact, the renovation project was nearing completion. Workers saw years of their efforts demolished in a matter of seconds—as well as the terrifying destruction of lives. However, the fact

The Pentagon Memorial, dedicated to those who lost their lives during the September 11 attacks, was opened on September 11, 2008.

that Wedge 1 was already partially vacated saved many other lives. The work to rebuild the Pentagon would continue.

Renovating the Pentagon

The renovation of the Pentagon began in 1998. The Pentagon had not had a major overhaul in its fifty-eight years, and the need was urgent. Much had changed since 1941. At the time the Pentagon was built there was one telephone for every three employees. By 1998, each person had two computers, one classified and one not classified, and a telephone. New wires had simply been laid on top of old ones. They ran above the ceiling panels, through floor conduits, and along hallways. In addition, the building did not meet current health and fire codes. It was not in total compliance with the Americans with Disabilities Act.

The building had been constructed in five parts, or wedges, connected to one another by expansion joints. The original plan was to work on one 1,000,000 square-foot (92,903 sq-m) wedge at a time. When the renovation started, all of the personnel who worked in Wedge 1 were moved into other offices in the Pentagon or into leased space. The contractors then took out everything down to the concrete slabs and columns. They removed 28,000,000 pounds (12,700,586 kilograms) of asbestos-contaminated material.

Safety Measures

Some of the innovations that kept the September 11 casualties down are steel beams that go through all five floors replacing the concrete columns. Kevlar cloth between the beams keeps debris from flying. The specially treated blast-proof glass windows stayed mostly intact even after the crash. Each of these special windows weighs 1,500 pounds (680 kg) and costs $10,000.

Other changes were designed to make the building safer and more efficient. Alterations to the ventilation system guard against nuclear, chemical, and biological attacks. The sprinkler system was updated. Added security features included putting glow-in-the-dark devices at floor level. The thinking behind this is that, in case of a fire, a person would be crawling and would not be looking for exit signs overhead.

The Pentagon was declared a historic structure in 1992, so the contractors were required to rebuild it to its original form. To replace the outside face, the contractor went back to the limestone quarry in Indiana where the original stone was quarried sixty years ago in order to match the original stone.

When engineers inspected the damaged part of the Pentagon they found small fractures in many of the columns. These were probably a result of the intense heat from the fire. The most severe damage was confined to Wedges 1 and 2. The contractor immediately began demolishing the damaged parts and began restoring Wedge 1.

The Reconstruction Team

Construction workers were inspired to rebuild the Pentagon to honor victims of the attack. They named the rebuilding The Phoenix Project, after the mythological bird that rose from ashes. Demolition of the damaged section was completed in just two months, removing ten thousand tons of debris. The renovation proceeded from the outside to the inside. Will Colsten, the manager of the project, said that this was not necessarily the most efficient way to do the work. However, from a national sense of pride, "it is more important to have the outside finished first." By January 2002,

The Pentagon construction site featured a digital countdown until the projected completion date of September 11, 2002.

more than one thousand employees had returned to their new offices. Although the official completion date of the project was set for September 11, 2002, most employees had returned back to work a month early, in August. However, smaller construction projects, including modernizing wiring systems, continued until 2011.

In order to rebuild the Pentagon under such time restraints, over six hundred people were employed on the Phoenix Project. For nearly one year, they worked in two ten-hour shifts a day, six days a week. Some workers protested when they were told they had to take two days off at Christmas. For the duration of the project, a digital clock counted down the seconds to the projected completion day.

In the early 1940s the Pentagon cost $50 million to build. The total cost to rebuild following the 2001 attack, including the rebuilding of the damaged area, is an estimated $500 million.

Investigating the ATTACK ON THE PENTAGON

While rebuilding the Pentagon, the symbol of the military strength of the United States, was an important goal following the attacks on September 11, another important goal was fighting the global war on terrorism.

The War Against Terrorism

In the first six months after the attacks, intelligence agencies foiled a number of terrorist attacks. These included attacks in Singapore and on American embassies in other parts of the world. In an interview with cable networks, Secretary of Defense Donald Rumsfeld said, "Our effort is worldwide, and it involves all elements of national power. It involves shutting down bank accounts, arresting people, law enforcement, maritime intercept of ships as a deterrent to see that they don't transfer terrorists or terrorist capabilities."

PENTAGON MEMORIAL

On September 11, 2008, the Pentagon Memorial, dedicated to all victims of the terrorist attack on the Pentagon, was officially opened. Designed by Julia Beckman and Keith Kaseman, the memorial honors the victims through 184 illuminated benches, which are arranged according to the victims' ages. Memorial benches for victims who were on Flight 77 are arranged according to the flight path of the plane, while benches for victims on the ground face the Pentagon's south facade. A small, lighted reflecting pool is located under each bench to encourage silent reflection on the national tragedy.

Rebuilding

United States intelligence agencies captured and questioned several members of the al-Qaeda network, including Abu Zubaydah, the network operations chief. For many years, Osama bin Laden and Taliban leader Mullah Omar remained at large. However, in 2011, Osama bin Laden was discovered and killed by US forces in a house in Abbottabad, Pakistan. This was the culmination of over ten years of hunting for the most well known terrorist in the world. Since then other masterminds of terrorist plots have also been captured or killed. Mullah Omar died in 2013.

The Pentagon Memorial features a bench and reflecting pool for each victim of the 2001 terrorist attack at the Pentagon.

Investigating the ATTACK ON THE PENTAGON

The war in Afghanistan drove the Taliban from power in Afghanistan and disrupted, but didn't eliminate, the al-Qaeda organization. The 2003 War in Iraq also aimed to disrupt global terrorist cells although evidence showed that there was no link between Iraq's president, Saddam Hussein, and the terrorist attacks of September 11. In the years since September 11, 2001, more global terrorist cells have been uncovered and more terrorist plots have been foiled. However, terrorism, and particularly Islamic extremism, remains a major problem that the United States government continues to battle. In particular, the rise of Islamist group the Islamic State (IS), which evolved from al-Qaeda in Iraq, has kept the global community on high alert. IS has surpassed al-Qaeda in terms of barbarous attacks and territory gained, although al-Qaeda and its direct affiliates continue to orchestrate attacks around the world.

The attacks on the United States on September 11, 2001, were a devastating reminder of the tragic consequences of hate. Through these attacks, as well as the global attacks that have followed in subsequent years, the American people have stood firm. They grieved and then set about the task of rebuilding and ridding the world of terrorism.

It has not been an easy task, but it is a necessary one that must continue.

Timeline

- **1989** Al-Qaeda is founded by Saudi Osama bin Laden to fight against Soviets in Afghanistan.

- **1993** The World Trade Center is bombed on February 26 by al-Qaeda members; six people are killed and over one thousand are injured.

- **1996** Osama bin Laden is expelled from Sudan and moves the al-Qaeda headquarters to Afghanistan.

- **1996** The Taliban gains power in Afghanistan.

- **1998** Bombs laid by al-Qaeda explode at US embassies in Kenya and Tanzania, killing 231 people.

- **2000** Two al-Qaeda suicide bombers attack the USS *Cole*, killing seventeen American sailors.

- **2001** Four planes are hijacked by al-Qaeda operatives and crashed into the World Trade Center, the Pentagon, and a field in Shanksville, Pennsylvania, killing nearly three thousand people. In October, American forces invade Afghanistan.

- **2002** Reconstruction on the Pentagon, named the Phoenix Project, is completed by the first anniversary of the September 11 attacks.

- **2003** American forces invade Iraq.

- **2004** Bombs planted by al-Qaeda members on commuter trains in Madrid, Spain, kill 190 people; In a video, Osama bin Laden claims direct responsibility for the 2001 attacks.

Timeline (continued)

- **2006** Zacarias Moussaoui is found guilty of terrorism charges in his role in the September 11 attacks and is sentenced to life in prison; al-Qaeda in Iraq is renamed the Islamic State in Iraq.

- **2008** The Pentagon Memorial is dedicated and opened to the public.

- **2011** Osama bin Laden is killed during a US Special Forces raid on his compound in Abottabad, Pakistan.

- **2013** The Islamic State in Iraq renames itself the Islamic State in Iraq and Syria (ISIS) after joining fighting in Syria's civil war.

- **2014** Now known as the Islamic State (IS), this terrorist organization gains territory in Iraq and American forces begin airstrikes against them.

- **2016** Iraqi forces, with American aid, begin an offensive to remove IS from their last stronghold in the Iraqi city of Mosul.

Glossary

Allah The word by which Muslims refer to the divine being.

appropriate Setting something aside for a particular purpose. This term often refers to a governmental body deciding where taxpayer's money will be spent.

classified Refers to sensitive items, such as papers and recordings, which can only be shown to certain people because of national security concerns.

condolences Expressions of sympathy to others.

cower To shrink in fear.

deploy Placing military forces where they will best be able to do their job.

dispatcher A person that oversees the departure of trains, planes, or buses.

exodus A large number of people leaving a certain place.

extremist A person who advocates radical religious or political measures.

fatwa An Islamic religious decree.

fuselage The main body of an airplane.

indictment The legal process by which a person is accused of a crime.

infidel A person who rejects the faith of a particular religion.

Islamic State of Iraq and Syria (ISIS) A terrorist group that emerged from al-Qaeda following the 2003 war in Iraq; also known as the Islamic State (IS).

jihad A holy war fought on behalf of Islam, or any crusade or struggle.

Kevlar A synthetic material that is remarkably strong; used in bulletproof vests, for example.

Koran The holy book of Islam.

militant Aggressive and ready to fight.

persevere To continue an action despite the difficulties faced.

simulator A machine with controls designed to imitate the operation of a vehicle or airplane.

For More Information

Federal Bureau of Investigation (FBI)
Department of Justice
935 Pennsylvania Avenue NW
Washington, DC 20535
(202) 324-3000
Website: http://www.fbi.gov

The FBI investigates national criminal activities, including terrorism and other major criminal threats, and is tasked with both intelligence and law enforcement responsibilities.

Federal Emergency Management Agency (FEMA)
500 C Street SW
Washington, DC 20472
(202) 566-1600
Website: http://www.fema.gov

FEMA is officially under the umbrella of the US Department of Homeland Security. Its primary task is to coordinate responses to disasters in the United States that cannot be handled by local authorities alone.

The National 9/11 Pentagon Memorial
PO Box 3879
Gaithersburg, MD 20885
(301) 740-3388
Website: http://pentagonmemorial.org

The Pentagon Memorial was created following the September 11 attacks to memorialize the victims of that day. A visitor education center helps to explain the historical significance of September 11, 2001.

For More Information

US Department of Defense (DOD)
1400 Defense Pentagon
Washington, DC 20301
(703) 571-3343
Website: http://www.defense.gov
The DOD is an executive-level department that governs American national security and all military branches; its headquarters are in the Pentagon.

US Department of Homeland Security (DHS)
12th and C Street SW
Washington, DC 20024
(202) 282-8000
Website: https://www.dhs.gov
Created after the September 11 attacks, the DHS provides a coordinated response to potential threats against the United States and works in border and cyber security, as well as in terrorism investigations and disaster prevention and management.

US Department of Justice (DOJ)
950 Pennsylvania Avenue NW
Washington, DC 20530
(202) 353-1555
Website: http://www.justice.gov
The DOJ is the executive-branch department tasked with enforcing the law and administering justice in the United States. It ensures fair trials for all American citizens and seeks appropriate punishments for convicted criminals.

US Department of State (DOS)
2201 C Street NW
Washington, DC 20520
(202) 647-4000
Website: http://www.state.gov
The DOS is responsible for overseeing the United States's foreign relations. It is charged with maintaining diplomatic relations and implementing US foreign policy.

Websites

Because of the changing nature of internet links, Rosen Publishing has developed an online list of websites related to the subject of this book. This site is updated regularly. Please use this link to access this list:

http://www.rosenlinks.com/TER21/pentagon

For Further Reading

Brown, Don. *America Is Under Attack: September 11, 2001: The Day the Towers Fell*. New York, NY: Flash Point, 2014.

Bush, George W. and Laura Bush. *Portraits of Courage: A Commander in Chief's Tribute to America's Warriors*. New York, NY: Crown, 2016.

Friedman, Lauri S. *Terrorism (Introducing Issues With* Opposing Viewpoints). New York, NY: Greenhaven Press, 2010.

Hillstrom, Kevin. *The September 11 Terrorist Attacks* (Defining Moments). Detroit, MI: Omnigraphics, Inc., 2012.

Owen, Mark and Kevin Maurer. *No Easy Day: The Firsthand Account of the Mission that Killed Osama Bin Laden*. New York, NY: Dutton, 2014.

Reeve, Simon. *The New Jackals*. Boston, MA: Northeastern University Press, 1999.

Rodgers, Tom. *Eleven*. Los Angeles, CA: Alto Nido Press, 2014.

Silverstein, Adam J. *Islamic History: A Very Short Introduction*. New York, NY: Oxford UP, 2010.

Tarshis, Lauren. *I Survived the Attacks of September 11, 2001*. New York, NY: Scholastic Paperbacks, 2012.

Vogel, Steve. *The Pentagon: A History*. New York, NY: Random House, 2008.

Zullo, Allan. *10 True Tales: Heroes of 9/11*. New York, NY: Scholastic Nonfiction, 2015.

Bibliography

ABC News. "Who Did It?" Republished on Freerepublic.com, January 9, 2002. http://www.freerepublic.com/focus/f-news/540045/posts.

"Al Qaeda." 2001. PBS *Frontline*. Retrieved October 27, 2016. http://www.pbs.org/wgbh/pages/frontline/shows/binladen/who/alqaeda.html.

"Attorney General Transcript, News Conference: DOJ to Seek Death Penalty Against Moussaoui." The Yale Law School Lillian Goldman Law Library, March 28, 2002. http://avalon.law.yale.edu/sept11/ashcroft_014.asp.

"Attorney General Transcript, News Conference Regarding Zacarias Moussaoui." The US Department of Justice, December 11, 2001. https://www.justice.gov/archive/ag/speeches/2001/agcrisisremarks12_11.htm.

Caruso, J. T. "Before the Subcommittee on International Operations and Terrorism, Committee of Foreign Relations." The Federal Bureau of Investigation, December 18, 2001. https://archives.fbi.gov/archives/news/testimony/al-qaeda-international.

Downey, Sarah. "Who Is Zacarias Moussaoui?" *Newsweek*, December 14, 2001.

"Fact Sheet: Terrorism." Federal Emergency Management Agency, September 23, 2001.

"Flight Data and Voice Recorders Found at Pentagon." *PBS, Online NewsHour*. Retrieved October 27, 2016. http://www.pbs.org/newshour/updates/terrorism-july-dec01-washington_09-14.

Goldberg, Alfred. *The Pentagon: The First Fifty Years*. Washington, DC: US Government Printing Office, 1992.

John, Tara. "Timeline: The Rise of ISIS." *Time*, October 9, 2015. http://time.com/4030714/isis-timeline-islamic-state.

Bibliography

Kaplan, David E., and Kevin Whitelaw. "The CEO of Terror, Inc." *US News & World Report*, October 1, 2001.

Mader, Robert P. "Tougher Pentagon to Rise." *Contractor*, July 2001.

McGeary, Johanna, and David van Biema. "The New Breed of Terrorism." *Time*, September 24, 2001.

"National Military Command Center." Federation of American Scientists. Retrieved November 2, 2016. www.fas.org/nuke/guide/usa/c3i/nmcc.htm

"Pentagon Attack Mementos Saved for Future Display." US Department of Defense. Retrieved October 27, 2016. http://archive.defense.gov/news/newsarticle.aspx?id=44403.

"Pentagon Renovation Program Management." *Parsons*. Retrieved November 3, 2016. https://www.parsons.com/projects/Pages/pentagon-renovation.aspx.

"Pentagon Renovation: The Phoenix Project." Pentagon Memorial website. Retrieved November 3, 2016. http://pentagonmemorial.org/learn/911-pentagon/pentagon-reconstruction-phoenix-project.

"The Pentagon." Brochure. Washington, DC: Office of the Assistant Secretary of Defense for Public Affairs.

Tanner, Victoria L. "Pentagon Gets Back to Business." *Design-Build Magazine*, December 2001.

Thomas, Evan. "Cracking the Terror Code." Newsweek, October 15, 2001.

"Translated Text: Hijackers' How-To." *CBS News*. Retrieved October 27, 2016. http://www.cbsnews.com/stories/2001/10/01/archive/main313163.shtml.

"U.S. War in Afghanistan: Timeline." *Council on Foreign Relations*. Retrieved November 3, 2016. http://www.cfr.org/afghanistan/us-war-afghanistan/p20018.

Index

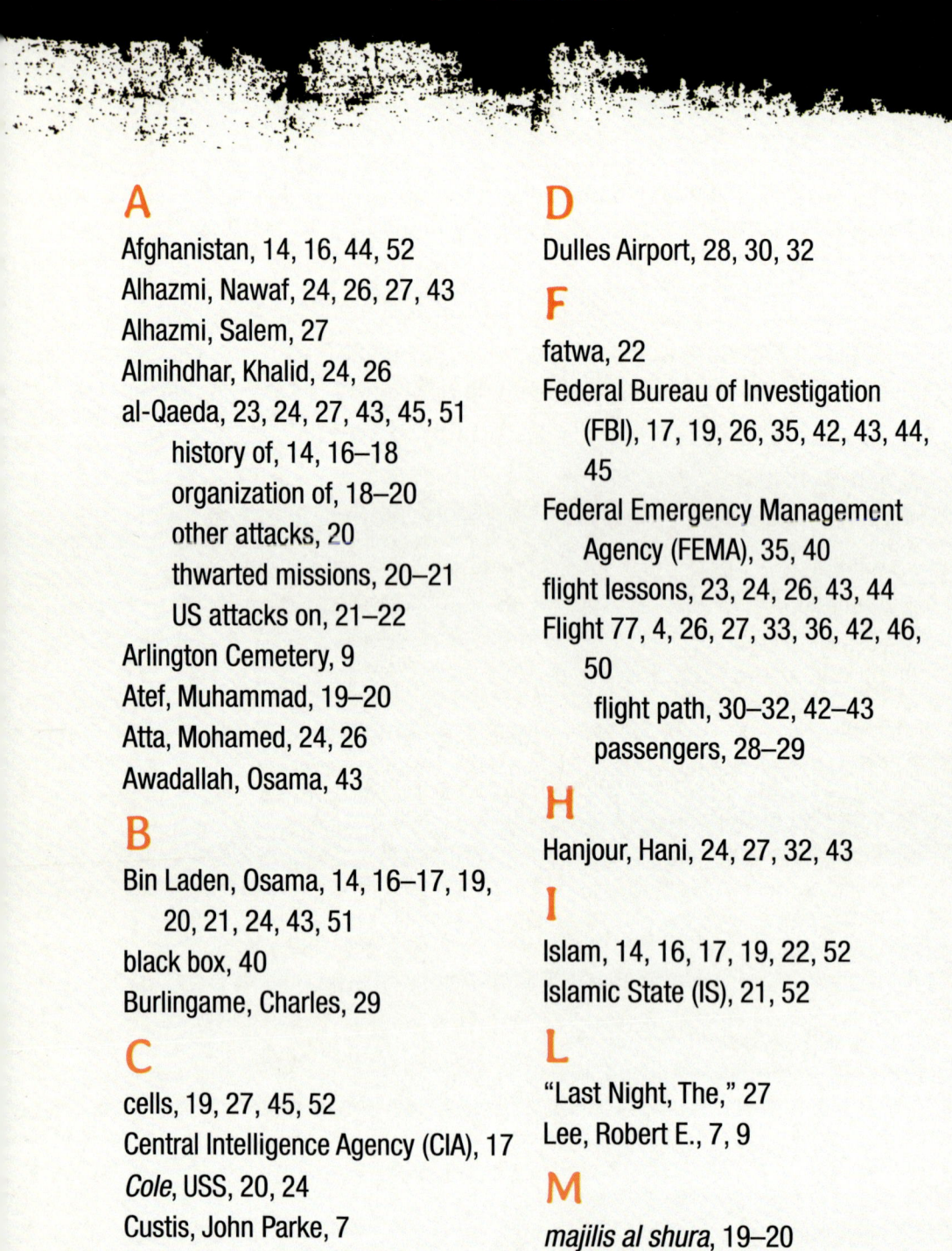

A
Afghanistan, 14, 16, 44, 52
Alhazmi, Nawaf, 24, 26, 27, 43
Alhazmi, Salem, 27
Almihdhar, Khalid, 24, 26
al-Qaeda, 23, 24, 27, 43, 45, 51
    history of, 14, 16–18
    organization of, 18–20
    other attacks, 20
    thwarted missions, 20–21
    US attacks on, 21–22
Arlington Cemetery, 9
Atef, Muhammad, 19–20
Atta, Mohamed, 24, 26
Awadallah, Osama, 43

B
Bin Laden, Osama, 14, 16–17, 19, 20, 21, 24, 43, 51
black box, 40
Burlingame, Charles, 29

C
cells, 19, 27, 45, 52
Central Intelligence Agency (CIA), 17
Cole, USS, 20, 24
Custis, John Parke, 7

D
Dulles Airport, 28, 30, 32

F
fatwa, 22
Federal Bureau of Investigation (FBI), 17, 19, 26, 35, 42, 43, 44, 45
Federal Emergency Management Agency (FEMA), 35, 40
flight lessons, 23, 24, 26, 43, 44
Flight 77, 4, 26, 27, 33, 36, 42, 46, 50
    flight path, 30–32, 42–43
    passengers, 28–29

H
Hanjour, Hani, 24, 27, 32, 43

I
Islam, 14, 16, 17, 19, 22, 52
Islamic State (IS), 21, 52

L
"Last Night, The," 27
Lee, Robert E., 7, 9

M
majilis al shura, 19–20

Index

Moqed, Majed, 27
Moussaoui, Zacarias, 43–45

N
National Military Command Center (NMCC), 33

O
Omar, Mohamed, 17, 51

P
Pakistan, 14, 16, 51
Pearl Harbor, 12, 36
Pentagon, attack on, 20
   hijackers last night before attack, 27
   impact, 4, 32–38
   investigation of, 42–43
   planning of, 23–24, 26–27
   rescue efforts, 34, 39–42
   suspects, 43–45
Pentagon, history of,
   facts and figures about, 11
   government plan for, 6–7, 9–10
   original construction of, 10–11, 13, 49
   reconstruction of, 46–49
Pentagon Memorial, 5, 50
Phoenix Project, 5, 48, 49

R
Raiss, Lofti, 43

Roosevelt, Franklin D., 9, 10
Rumsfeld, Donald, 32, 33, 38, 50

S
Salmi, Faisal Michael Al, 43
Saudi Arabia, 14, 17, 24, 26
Somalia, 14
Somervell, Brehon, 6, 9
Sudan, 16, 17

T
Taliban, 17, 52
terrorism, war against, 50–52

U
urban search and rescue teams (US&R), 40, 42
US Department of Defense, 4, 33

W
Woodrun, Clifton, 9
World Trade Center
   1993 bombing, 17
   September 11 attack, 20, 24, 26, 31, 32, 50, 52
World War II, 6, 13

About the Authors

Lena Koya is a writer and scholar who lives in New York with her family. She researches literature about the 2003 Iraq War and enjoys writing about current events for teenagers.

Carolyn Gard is a former teacher and writer who writes mainly for teenagers. In addition, she does research for members of the Colorado State Legislature. She lives in Boulder, Colorado, where she enjoys hiking with her German shepherds.

Photo Credits

Cover, p. 1 Everett Historical/Shutterstock.com; back cover and interior pages background aleksandr hunta/Shutterstock.com (smoke); p. 5 Frontpage/Shutterstock.com; p. 7 © iStockphoto.com/Mlucas; p. 8 New York Post Archives/The New York Post/Getty Images; p. 12 Myron Davis/The LIFE Picture Collection/Getty Images; p. 15 AFP/Getty Images; p. 18 Stacey Walsh Rosenstock/Alamy Stock Photo; p. 20 0851/Gamma-Rapho/Getty Images; p. 23 REUTERS/Alamy Stock Photo; p. 25 Mai/The LIFE Images Collection/Getty Images; p. 28 U.S. Navy/Getty Images; p. 30 Douglas Graham/CQ-Roll Call Group/Getty Images; p. 34 Brooks Kraft/Corbis Historical/Getty Images; p. 35 Greg Whitesell/Getty Images; p. 37 FEMA/Getty Images; p. 39 US Navy Photo/Alamy Stock Photo; p. 41 Inked Pixels/Shutterstock.com; p. 44 Chip Somodevilla/Getty Images; p. 46 Vacclav/Shutterstock.com; p. 49 Mark Wilson/Getty Images; p. 51 Tom Williams/CQ-Roll Call Group/Getty Images.

Designer: Nicole Russo-Duca; Editor: Elizabeth Schmermund; Photo Researcher: Elizabeth Schmermund